Thinking Critically: Abortion

Other titles in the *Thinking Critically* series include:

**Thinking Critically:
Abortion**

Christine Wilcox

ReferencePoint
Press®

San Diego, CA

© 2018 ReferencePoint Press, Inc.
Printed in the United States

For more information, contact:
ReferencePoint Press, Inc.
PO Box 27779
San Diego, CA 92198
www.ReferencePointPress.com

Picture Credits:
Charts and graphs by Maury Aaseng

LIBRARY OF CONGRESS CATALOGING-IN-PUBLICATION DATA

Name: Wilcox, Christine, author.
Title: Thinking Critically: Abortion/by Christine Wilcox.
Description: San Diego, CA : ReferencePoint Press, Inc., [2018] | Series: Thinking Critically | Includes bibliographical references and index.
Identifiers: LCCN 2016052613 (print) | LCCN 2017005697 (ebook) | ISBN 9781682822616 (hardback) | ISBN 9781682822623 (eBook)
Subjects: LCSH: Abortion—Juvenile literature.
Classification: LCC HQ767 .W53 2018 (print) | LCC HQ767 (ebook) | DDC 362.1988/8--dc23
LC record available at https://lccn.loc.gov/2016052613

Contents

Foreword

"Literacy is the most basic currency of the knowledge economy we're living in today." Barack Obama (at the time a senator from Illinois) spoke these words during a 2005 speech before the American Library Association. One question raised by this statement is: What does it mean to be a literate person in the twenty-first century?

E.D. Hirsch Jr., author of *Cultural Literacy: What Every American Needs to Know*, answers the question this way: "To be culturally literate is to possess the basic information needed to thrive in the modern world. The breadth of the information is great, extending over the major domains of human activity from sports to science."

But literacy in the twenty-first century goes beyond the accumulation of knowledge gained through study and experience and expanded over time. Now more than ever literacy requires the ability to sift through and evaluate vast amounts of information and, as the authors of the Common Core State Standards state, to "demonstrate the cogent reasoning and use of evidence that is essential to both private deliberation and responsible citizenship in a democratic republic."

The *Thinking Critically* series challenges students to become discerning readers, to think independently, and to engage and develop their skills as critical thinkers. Through a narrative-driven, pro/con format, the series introduces students to the complex issues that dominate public discourse—topics such as gun control and violence, social networking, and medical marijuana. All chapters revolve around a single, pointed question such as Can Stronger Gun Control Measures Prevent Mass Shootings?, or Does Social Networking Benefit Society?, or Should Medical Marijuana Be Legalized? This inquiry-based approach introduces student researchers to core issues and concerns on a given topic. Each chapter includes one part that argues the affirmative and one part that argues the negative—all written by a single author. With the single-author format the predominant arguments for and against an issue can be synthesized into clear, accessible discussions supported by details and evidence including relevant facts, direct quotes, current examples, and statistical illustrations. All volumes include focus questions to guide students as they read each pro/con discussion, a list of key facts, and an annotated list of related organizations and websites for conducting further research.

The authors of the Common Core State Standards have set out the particular qualities that a literate person in the twenty-first century must have. These include the ability to think independently, establish a base of knowledge across a wide range of subjects, engage in open-minded but discerning reading and listening, know how to use and evaluate evidence, and appreciate and understand diverse perspectives. The new *Thinking Critically* series supports these goals by providing a solid introduction to the study of pro/con issues.

Abortion

During the final presidential debate in 2016, candidates Hillary Clinton and Donald Trump described their stance on abortions that take place late in pregnancy. "The kinds of [abortion] cases that fall at the end of pregnancy are often the most heartbreaking, painful decisions for families to make," Clinton said. "I do not think the US government should be stepping in and making those most personal of decisions."[1] Trump disagreed, characterizing late-term abortion in the following way: "You can take the baby and rip the baby out of the womb in the ninth month, on the final day, and that's not acceptable."[2] Their statements set off yet another national debate on abortion, in part because they capture the essence of this controversial subject: When it comes to legislating abortion, whose rights are primary, a pregnant woman or the fetus she carries?

This debate has raged in American society since 1973, when the US Supreme Court handed down its landmark decision on abortion in the case known as *Roe v. Wade*. The court determined that a woman's decision to seek an abortion was a constitutional right until fetal viability, or the point at which a fetus can survive with medical intervention outside the womb (usually defined as twenty-four weeks). After that point, states are permitted to regulate abortion as long as they make an exception to protect the life and health of the mother and the laws do not create substantial barriers to abortion access.

Understanding Abortion

The language that surrounds abortion tends to be highly biased and sometimes misleading, so it is important to define the terminology of fetal development and abortion.

Before birth, a human offspring goes through several stages of development. The first is referred to as fertilization or conception—the point at which an egg and sperm join to create a single cell, or zygote, which has a complete and unique set of human deoxyribonucleic acid (DNA). When the zygote begins to divide, it is called an embryo. At nine weeks, after all major body organs exist in a rudimentary form, it is called a fetus. In nonmedical language, it is common to use the term *fetus* to refer to human offspring at any point before birth, unless a specific stage of development is being discussed.

Abortion is the termination of a pregnancy that results in the death of a fetus. (Spontaneous abortion—when the fetus dies on its own—is usually referred to as miscarriage.) Several methods of abortion are commonly practiced in the United States. A medical abortion can usually be performed up until week nine of pregnancy. Two drugs must be taken in sequence; the first causes the fetus to detach from the uterine wall and die, and the second causes the uterus to contract and expel the fetus. A surgical abortion can take several forms. A vacuum aspiration abortion can be performed in the first twelve weeks of pregnancy, though some providers perform it up until week sixteen. In this procedure a powerful vacuum removes the fetus, causing its death. Once vacuum aspiration is no longer possible, abortion is generally performed by dilation and evacuation (D&E). Because the fetus is too large to be removed whole without risking injury to a woman's cervix, it is removed in pieces with forceps, which causes its death. Toward the end of pregnancy, an induction abortion must be performed. In this rare procedure, the fetus is injected with a chemical that kills it, and then labor is induced to expel it. Another technique known as partial-birth abortion (also called intact D&E) was banned in the United States in 2003.

According to the Guttmacher Institute, a reproductive rights research organization, of the 1.06 million abortions performed in the United

> "The kinds of [abortion] cases that fall at the end of pregnancy are often the most heartbreaking, painful decisions for families to make."[1]
>
> — Hillary Clinton, 2016 Democratic presidential candidate

US Abortion Rate Reaches Lowest Level in Years

A Centers for Disease Control and Prevention (CDC) annual report, released in November 2016, reveals that the number and rate of abortions in the United States has fallen to the lowest level in many years. According to the report, between 2004 and 2013 the total number of reported abortions decreased 20 percent; the rate of reported abortions decreased 21 percent; and the ratio of reported abortions decreased 17 percent. The abortion rate for 2013 alone was 12.5 abortions per one thousand women (aged fifteen to forty-four), a figure that is half the rate of 25 recorded in 1980. To arrive at these numbers, the report used data from forty-seven states that provided abortion statistics to the CDC each year during that period. The report cites several possible reasons for the decline. These include a large drop in teen pregnancies, expanded coverage of birth control costs by health care plans, and more effective methods of birth control.

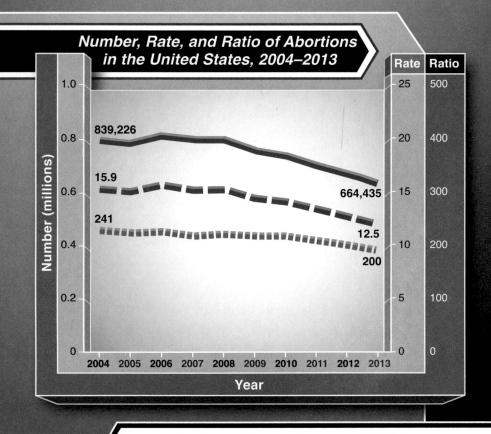

Source: Tara C. Jatlaoui et al., "Abortion Surveillance—United States, 2013," MMWR Surveillance Summaries, vol. 65, no. 12, November 25, 2016. www.cdc.gov.

States in 2011 (the most recent date for which comprehensive statistics are available), 91 percent occurred in the first thirteen weeks, 7.2 percent occurred between fourteen and twenty weeks, and 1.3 percent occurred at or after twenty-one weeks. The focus of most abortion controversy is on second trimester D&E abortions, which can legally be performed on healthy fetuses. Studies have found that women who have D&E abortions sometimes do so because barriers to abortion—including financial ones—prevent them from having an abortion earlier. Other women have D&E abortions because of health issues or because they learn of fetal abnormalities late in the pregnancy. Induction abortion is almost always performed because of severe fetal abnormalities or grave health risks to the mother. When an abortion is performed after fetal viability, it is usually referred to as a late-term abortion, regardless of the method used.

Who Gets Abortions?

Women who have abortions come from all walks of life; however, poor and minority women are more likely to have abortions. In 2014, 61 percent of women who had abortions were members of minority groups, and 49 percent had incomes below the federal poverty level (up from 42 percent in 2008). More than half already had one or more children, and three-quarters cited financial issues as a reason for seeking abortion.

In recent years the number of abortions decreased by 13 percent, from 1.21 million in 2008 to 1.06 million in 2011. Between 2008 and 2014 the proportion of teenagers seeking abortion dropped sharply by 32 percent. However, live births also declined by 40 percent, indicating that fewer teens are getting pregnant overall.

Public Opinion

According to a 2015 Gallup Poll, 50 percent of adults identify themselves as pro-choice (those who tend to support legalized abortion or oppose restrictions on it), and 44 percent identify as pro-life (those who tend to oppose abortion or prefer restrictions on it). However, many people who identify as pro-choice also believe that *Roe v. Wade* is too permissive. For instance, a 2016 survey by the Marist Institute for Public Opinion found that only 22 percent believed abortion should be legal in the second or third trimester. This indicates that the public tends to favor the rights of the fetus over the rights of the mother as the fetus becomes more mature.

Most people believe abortion should remain legal in the first trimester. Most also believe abortion should be permitted at any stage to protect the life of the mother. Fewer people agree with the provision of *Roe v. Wade* that says that post-viability abortion is permitted to protect the health of the mother, which includes non-life-threatening complications to pregnancy. According to a 2016 Pew Research Center poll, only 16 percent of adults believed abortion should be illegal in all cases, while 24 percent believed abortion should be legal in all cases.

The Battle in the States

In recent years pro-life advocates have focused their efforts on passing state laws that restrict abortion—a strategy that has been remarkably successful. Since 2010, 334 new laws have been passed by the states, which constitutes 30 percent of all state abortion laws passed since 1973. Some laws ban abortion after a certain point in pregnancy, in most cases because the state argues that a fetus can feel pain earlier than the point of viability. Some laws prohibit the use of state funds for abortion. Others institute mandatory waiting periods or counseling requirements, which states say are to ensure that women have time to fully consider the information provided about abortion. Some laws state that minors seeking abortions must either get consent from their parents or at least notify them about their decision to abort. Finally, some laws, known as targeted regulation of abortion providers (TRAP) laws, require abortion providers and facilities to meet strict standards of care—standards that pro-life advocates say protect women's health but pro-choice advocates say are unnecessary or even unrelated to abortion provision. As a result of TRAP laws, 162 clinics closed between 2011 and 2016.

Pro-choice advocates assert that all of these laws have the single aim of limiting women's legal right to abortion. They also say that these laws disproportionately affect teens and lower-income women, who are forced to travel long distances to the remaining open clinics (often two or more times to comply with waiting period restrictions). Many of these women cannot afford to pay for an abortion out of pocket; or in the case of teens, they are afraid to tell their parents they are pregnant. The result is that many women get abortions later than they would like or are forced to give birth to unwanted children. Pro-life advocates argue that such laws are designed to protect women and allow them to put the time and thought into what could be the biggest decision of their life.

The Future of Abortion in the United States

Most experts agree that the future of abortion in the United States will be determined in the federal courts. For instance, in 2016 the Supreme Court made a landmark ruling that determined that Texas's restrictive TRAP laws placed an undue burden on women seeking an abortion. In his opening argument, Solicitor General Don Verrilli said, "This law closes most abortion facilities in the state, puts extreme stress on the few facilities that remain open, and exponentially increases the obstacles confronting women who seek abortions."[3] Pro-choice advocates hope the ruling will result in fewer TRAP laws in the future.

The issue of abortion is so complex that it is sure to be controversial for years to come. Questions such as whether a fetus has a right to life, whether a woman can be forced to support a fetus with her body, and whether abortion is a social good or a moral failing will continue to be debated as long as unwanted pregnancy is a reality. However, considering that almost half of pregnancies in the United States are unintended, it is likely that abortion—at least under some circumstances—will remain legal for the foreseeable future.

Chapter One

Is a Fetus a Person with a Right to Life?

A Fetus Is a Person with a Right to Life

- Scientists agree that human life is created at conception.
- A developing human is just as entitled to basic human rights as a fully developed one; human rights do not depend on the way a human looks or functions.
- Society already recognizes fetuses as having certain rights.

The Debate at a Glance

A Fetus Is Not a Person and Its Right to Life Is Not Absolute

- Neither science nor philosophy support the idea that a person is created at conception.
- Society does not view a fetus as having the same status as a person.
- In most cases society already places more value on a woman's right to life than on a fetus's because both society and the law value the right to control one's own body.

A Fetus Is a Person with a Right to Life

"A person is a person, whether they're unborn or whether they're out of the womb. Their personhood is clearly indicated by the biology that we know from conception forward."

—Mike Huckabee, Christian minister and former governor of Arkansas

Quoted in Personhood USA, "Huckabee: 5th and 14th Amendments Guarantee Personhood for All," August 18, 2015. www.personhood.com.

Consider these questions as you read:

1. How does this essay define *personhood*? Use examples from the text in your answer.
2. Taking into account the facts and ideas presented in this discussion, how persuasive is the argument that personhood begins at conception? Which arguments are strongest and why?
3. What do you think is meant by *dehumanization*, and how does it relate to abortion?

Editor's note: The discussion that follows presents common arguments made in support of this perspective, reinforced by facts, quotes, and examples taken from various sources.

The most fundamental argument in the abortion debate is whether a fetus is a person with a fundamental right to life. *Roe v. Wade* grants a fetus the rights of personhood at birth, as if moving through the birth canal somehow makes a human life worth protecting. However, both science and common sense confirm that personhood does not begin at birth—or at any other stage of development in the womb. A person is created at conception, when human life begins. It is at this point that the fundamental right to life must be protected by law.

Human Beings Are Created at Conception

There is no doubt that a fertilized egg, or zygote, is both alive and human. From its first moment of existence, it has an individual human nature encoded in its DNA. As a newly formed human at the first stage of development, it is by definition a human being—a fact that scientists have known for decades. For instance, Keith Moore, a prominent embryologist, writes, "[The zygote], formed by the union of an oocyte and a sperm, is the beginning of a new human being."[4] This position is widely accepted even by the pro-choice establishment. For instance, Bernard Nathanson, cofounder of the powerful abortion advocacy group NARAL Pro-Choice America, writes, "There is simply no doubt that even the early embryo is a human being."[5]

Because there is widespread agreement that a human being comes into existence at conception, pro-choice advocates often justify abortion by arguing that a human being is not the same thing as a person. In doing so, however, they create an unacceptable situation in which some human beings have value and others do not.

Personhood Does Not Depend on Appearance or Functionality

What is the difference between a human being and a person? In the abortion debate, pro-choice advocates say it involves appearance and functionality. Because an embryo does not look, function, or think like a person, they say it is not one. For instance, Planned Parenthood often characterizes an embryo as a "blob of tissue"[6] that cannot think or feel.

Using appearance or functionality to assign value to a human being is a dangerous practice that has had horrific consequences. Historically, nonwhite people were not regarded as persons, which was used to justify their enslavement and slaughter. African American slaves in the United States were once legally considered to be three-fifths of a person. In 1881 legal scholar George Canfield stated, "an Indian is not a person within the meaning of the Constitution."[7] Functionality was also once linked to human worth. Early in the twentieth century, more than thirty US states had laws that required people with certain disabilities to be

16

Most Americans Believe a Fetus Is a Person

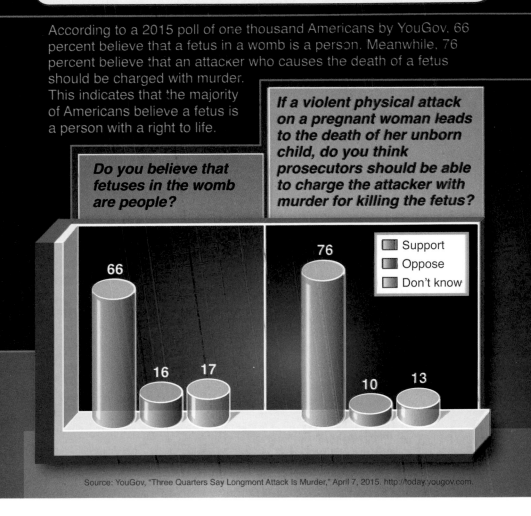

According to a 2015 poll of one thousand Americans by YouGov, 66 percent believe that a fetus in a womb is a person. Meanwhile, 76 percent believe that an attacker who causes the death of a fetus should be charged with murder. This indicates that the majority of Americans believe a fetus is a person with a right to life.

Do you believe that fetuses in the womb are people?

If a violent physical attack on a pregnant woman leads to the death of her unborn child, do you think prosecutors should be able to charge the attacker with murder for killing the fetus?

- Support
- Oppose
- Don't know

66

16   17

76

10   13

Source: YouGov, "Three Quarters Say Longmont Attack Is Murder," April 7, 2015. http://today.yougov.com.

forcibly sterilized so they would not reproduce. In Germany, about two hundred thousand handicapped people, many of them children, were killed between 1940 and 1945 because the Nazi Party considered them "unworthy of life."[8]

In all of these cases, people with untraditional appearances or functionalities were dehumanized—a term that means to characterize a person as less than human. Dehumanization is frequently used to make it easier to exploit, harm, or kill others. Pro-choice activists who characterize an embryo as merely a "blob of tissue" are dehumanizing a human being based on its appearance and functionality. Not only does defining a human's worth by appearance and function dehumanize fetuses, it dehumanizes anyone with a physical birth defect or less-than-optimal functionality, including the disabled. It even dehumanizes healthy infants. This type of thinking is what has allowed pro-choice philosopher Peter Singer to claim that infants are not persons. "Human babies are not born self-aware, or capable of grasping that they exist over time," he writes. "They are not persons. . . . The life of a newborn is of less value than the life of a pig, a dog, or a chimpanzee."[9] His statements show how equating personhood with functionality can dehumanize an infant to the point that it is regarded as less valuable than an animal.

Personhood Does Not Depend on Viability

Some people believe that personhood begins when a fetus is viable, or able to survive outside the womb. This is affirmed by *Roe v. Wade*, which somewhat protects a fetus from abortion once it is viable (though it does not grant it full rights of personhood until birth). Before this point, a fetus is essentially the nonhuman property of the woman, and whether she carries it to term or aborts it is entirely her choice.

The problem with using viability as a definition of personhood is that it is an arbitrary measure that has less to do with an intrinsic human quality and more to do with advancements in medical technology. According to Edward Bell, a neonatologist at the University of Iowa Children's Hospital, because of advancements in medicine that can keep premature babies alive much earlier than in the past, "the threshold [of viability] has decreased by one week for every decade."[10] When Bell first began practicing in the 1970s, it was not really possible for a newborn to live outside the womb until twenty-six weeks. Today advances

> "Technologies change, babies do not. Surely we cannot believe that the sophistication of life support systems determines the reality or worth of human life!"[11]
>
> —San Antonio Coalition for Life

in life-support apparatuses and other technologies could allow a preterm infant as young as twenty-two weeks to survive. This means that a fetus conceived in 1978 would become a "person" at twenty-six weeks, while one conceived in 2017 would become a person at twenty-two weeks. According to the San Antonio Coalition for Life, this is illogical: "Technologies change, babies do not. Surely we cannot believe that the sophistication of life support systems determines the reality or worth of human life!"[11]

It seems clear that there is no stage of gestation in which a fetus suddenly becomes a person and therefore intrinsically valuable. This is because *all* living human beings are intrinsically valuable, regardless of their appearance, functionality, or developmental stage. This is a fundamental belief of all civilized societies, which pass laws that protect human beings no matter what they look like, what they are able to do, or whether medical technology can keep them alive. According to Personhood USA, a pro-life organization, "Living human beings are valuable because of what they are, not because of some arbitrary attribute that comes in varying degrees and which may be gained or lost during their lifetimes."[12]

> "It's lunacy. No other class of person is given value by the person who harms them."[14]
>
> —Brian Fisher, president of Human Coalition

Society Already Recognizes That Fetuses Are Persons

The irony of this debate is that fetuses are already recognized as persons with a right to life. The Unborn Victims of Violence Act, a federal law passed in 2004, states that if a fetus is killed during the commission of a federal crime, that fetus is a legal victim and the perpetrator can be prosecuted for murder. As of 2016 thirty-eight states have similar fetal homicide laws. The language in these laws is modeled on the federal law, which refers to a fetus in any stage of development as the "child in utero."[13] Fetal homicide laws tend to get passed unanimously and enjoy tremendous support from the public. Clearly, society already believes that a child in utero at any stage of development is indeed a person.

Fetal homicide laws make it clear that, in cases of violence against pregnant women, a fetus has a constitutionally protected right to life. Yet when it comes to abortion—the ultimate violence—the fetus's life has no value. "It's lunacy," asserts Brian Fisher, the cofounder and president of the pro-life group Human Coalition. "No other class of person is given value by the person who harms them."[14]

Science has unanimously asserted that human life begins at conception, and society believes that human life has intrinsic worth—worth that does not depend on appearance or function. It is time that society extends that value to all human life and grants fetuses the rights and protections of personhood.

A Fetus Is Not a Person and Its Right to Life Is Not Absolute

"Tammy lost her liberty, her privacy, her medical decision making. . . . Every right that we associate with being a person was taken from her. All in the name of protecting a 14-week-old fetus."

—Lawyer Sara Ainsworth about her pregnant client Tammy Loertscher

Quoted in Ada Calhoun, "Jailed for Using Drugs While Pregnant," *Atlantic*, October 12, 2015. www.theatlantic.com.

Consider these questions as you read:

1. How convincing is the argument that a fetus is not a person? Explain your answer using examples from the text.
2. How does the essay explain the apparent contradiction between abortion laws and fetal homicide laws?
3. There is very little difference, biologically, between a nine-month-old fetus and a newborn. In your opinion, is one of them a person? Both? Neither? Use the text to support your answer.

Editor's note: The discussion that follows presents common arguments made in support of this perspective, reinforced by facts, quotes, and examples taken from various sources.

Scientists have long known that biological life begins at conception—a fertilized egg is both alive and human. But this life is not the same thing as being a "person" as society commonly defines it. Personhood—the belief that a person is created at conception—is not supported by science or philosophy. A fetus's life is not more important than the life of the woman who carries it. And as long as that life is inside a woman's body, its rights are never absolute.

Science Does Not Support Personhood

Despite the claims of the personhood movement, science does not support the idea that a fertilized egg is a person. At conception, a human egg and sperm form a single cell that contains newly formed DNA. But just like a recipe is not a meal and a blueprint is not a building, DNA is not a person; it is merely the instructions to create a person.

In fact, the instructions can even create two or more persons. An embryo can split into identical twins in the first week after fertilization. Twin embryos have identical DNA, but they do not become identical people—identical twins have their own personalities and identities. In addition, the vast majority of twin embryos are reabsorbed into the uterine lining or into the surviving twin. Thus, not only can DNA split to form two embryos (or more, in rare cases), it can recombine into a single embryo. This makes it clear that the creation of new DNA is not the same thing as the creation of a new person. As journalist Adam Gopnik explains, "A fertilized egg or embryo is not some freeze-dried essence of human but a complex set of potentials that need many, many conditions to develop into a human being."[15]

The science of human reproduction also makes it clear that nature does not value human embryos in the same way that our society values people. Personhood advocates often lament that millions of persons have been murdered through abortion. However, they do not acknowledge that many millions more have been aborted by women's bodies—most times without their knowledge. "There's an incredibly high rate of fertilized eggs that don't implant,"[16] says Diane Horvath-Cosper, an obstetrician and gynecologist (ob-gyn) in Washington, DC. Studies show that up to 80 percent of all zygotes and early embryos do not implant in the uterine lining, and many that do implant will spontaneously abort. This is a natural process of selection that nature imposes on reproduction to ensure that only the healthiest fetuses in the healthiest environments survive. "Virtually all sexual reproduction, whether of plants or animals,

> "A fertilized egg or embryo is not some freeze-dried essence of human but a complex set of potentials."[15]
>
> —Journalist Adam Gopnik

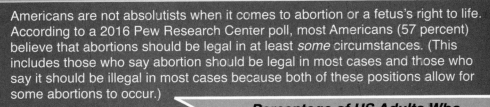

Americans are not absolutists when it comes to abortion or a fetus's right to life. According to a 2016 Pew Research Center poll, most Americans (57 percent) believe that abortions should be legal in at least *some* circumstances. (This includes those who say abortion should be legal in most cases and those who say it should be illegal in most cases because both of these positions allow for some abortions to occur.)

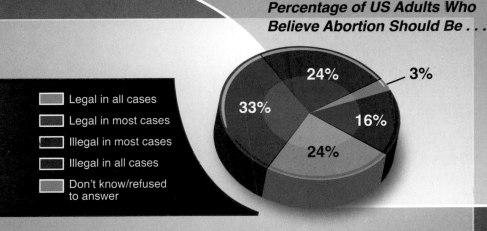

Percentage of US Adults Who Believe Abortion Should Be . . .

- Legal in all cases
- Legal in most cases
- Illegal in most cases
- Illegal in all cases
- Don't know/refused to answer

24% 3%
33% 16%
24%

Source: Pew Research Center, "Public Opinion on Abortion," April 8, 2016. www.pewforum.org.

follows a similar pattern, with lots of false starts built into the equation and a fertility rate that compensates," explains psychologist Valerie Tarico. "No farmer expects every seed to grow."[17] In other words, nature discards embryos far too often for them to be intrinsically valuable.

Most doctors agree with this thinking. The American Congress of Obstetricians and Gynecologists, which represents more than fifty-five thousand doctors who specialize in female reproduction, officially opposes personhood legislation. In fact, even scientists who believe that persons are created at conception acknowledge that their beliefs are not supported by science. As biologist and bioethicist Dianne N. Irving states, "The question of when a human person begins is a philosophical question not a scientific question."[18]

Philosophy Does Not Support Personhood

Philosophers tend to equate personhood with traits associated with what it means to be human. According to philosopher Daniel Fincke, "Personhood emerges through a large cluster of functional capacities that have as their minimal basis things like rationality, emotions, sociability, and self awareness." Fincke says that these are the things that make humans separate individuals with unique thoughts, feelings, memories, and opinions. When these things are lost, humans cease to be persons. "When someone irrevocably loses all of her mental, emotional, social, and consciousness powers, she is effectively dead. The person is gone; even if her biological body can still be kept working," he explains. "At that point we let the body go and we grieve the lost person."[19]

Personhood also depends on an entity's ability to interact with the world. According to Tarico, even a fetus in later stages of gestation needs to experience life outside the womb in order to distinguish itself as an individual that exists apart from its mother. As she explains, "The individual person emerges through interaction between the organism and the environment. Without stimulation the human brain doesn't form a mind."[20] Until this happens, a fetus merely has the potential to become a person. This is why most philosophers assert that the process of becoming a person does not begin in a meaningful way until after birth.

Society Does Not Recognize Fetuses as Persons

The norms and conventions of American society support these ideas. For instance, until a human being exists outside the womb, it is not counted in censuses and cannot have a legal name or a Social Security number. Its age is calculated from date of birth, not from date of conception, and if a fetus dies, it is not given a death certificate. Tax law does not allow a pregnant woman to declare a fetus as a dependent for tax purposes, even though she has to expend resources to support the pregnancy. In fact, as far as society is concerned, a fetus is a physical part of its mother because it lives inside her body and depends on her—and only her—for its survival. The majority of US voters agree with these sentiments, because each time a personhood measure has been on the ballot, voters have overwhelmingly rejected it.

On the other hand, Americans do believe that in most instances a woman has the right to end her pregnancy. Polls consistently find that the vast majority of adults believe a woman should be allowed to end a pregnancy in its first three months in cases of rape or incest or when her own life or health is in jeopardy. Society also supports a woman's choice to carry a pregnancy to term. This is why fetal homicide laws get so much support from the public. These laws state that if a fetus dies during an attack on its mother, the attacker is guilty of murder. They support a woman's choice to remain pregnant by making it a crime to harm her fetus. In short, society gives a woman's rights precedent over those of her fetus. Society believes that a woman has a right to choose, and it creates laws that support her choice.

> "Without stimulation the human brain doesn't form a mind."[20]
>
> —Psychologist Valerie Tarico

This is because Americans believe in body autonomy—the right to control what happens to one's own body. Except in the area of abortion law, there are no US federal laws that require people to use their bodies to sustain others. If a child needs a lifesaving bone marrow donation, no one can be forced to provide it. Lifesaving organ donation is also never required, even after death, though millions of lives would be saved if it were. Even if a person causes a child to be gravely injured, that person is not legally required to donate his or her blood to save the child's life. US law respects a person's autonomy over his or her body. This is why society generally believes that a woman has the right to refuse to support a fetus with her body, even if it means the fetus will die.

According to science, reason, and society, a fetus is not a person. It has the potential to become a person, but whether it fulfills that potential must be left up to the mother—who is already a person under the law and already has the right to control what happens to her body. *Roe v. Wade* already acknowledges that fetuses have some rights after viability. But those rights are not absolute, and they should never override the rights of women.

Chapter Two

Is Abortion Harmful to Women?

Abortion Is Harmful to Women

- Abortion carries very real risks, including the risk of death.
- Women who choose abortion are more likely to suffer serious mental health disorders.
- Choosing adoption allows women to protect their own health and well-being.

The Debate at a Glance

Abortion Is Not Harmful to Women

- Abortion is much safer than pregnancy, both physically and mentally.
- Having the option of abortion allows women to take better care of the family they already have.
- Reproductive choice allows women to plan their futures and reach their potential.

Abortion Is Harmful to Women

"Abortion . . . is turning women against their own uniqueness. . . . Abortion is definitely a war on women."

—Maria McFadden Maffucci, editor of the *Human Life Review*

Quoted in Stella Morabito, "*Human Life Review*: Forty Years of Fighting for Human Life and Dignity," *Federalist*, October 21, 2014. http://thefederalist.com.

Consider these questions as you read:

1. Taking into account the facts and ideas presented in this discussion, evaluate the argument that abortion may not be safer than childbirth. Do you agree or disagree? Explain your answer.
2. What are some of the reasons given for why women who have had abortions are at an increased risk of mental health problems? Can you think of any additional reasons?
3. Considering abortion's health risks, why do you think more women do not choose adoption?

Editor's note: The discussion that follows presents common arguments made in support of this perspective, reinforced by facts, quotes, and examples taken from various sources.

To many women facing an unexpected pregnancy, abortion may seem like the easy answer. However, abortion carries serious short- and long-term risks to women—risks that are often minimized by the abortion industry. In contrast, adoption offers women a way to avoid these risks while honoring their unique role in the creation of life.

Abortion May Not Be Safer than Childbirth

Pro-choice advocates often say that women are fourteen times more likely to die for reasons associated with childbirth than from abortion.

A 2016 Catholic University of America study found strong links between abortion and mental health disorders in women who have undergone the procedure. The study, which tracked the mental health history of 8,005 women for thirteen years, found that those who had an abortion had almost double the risk of developing mental health disorders (45 percent) than those who had experienced an involuntary pregnancy loss, or miscarriage (24 percent). Mental health disorders observed included depression and suicidal thoughts, anxiety, and drug and alcohol abuse and addiction. The study indicates that abortion causes significant psychological harm to women.

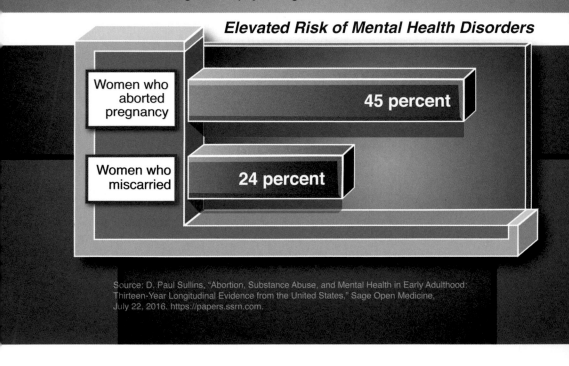

Elevated Risk of Mental Health Disorders

Women who aborted pregnancy — 45 percent

Women who miscarried — 24 percent

Source: D. Paul Sullins, "Abortion, Substance Abuse, and Mental Health in Early Adulthood: Thirteen-Year Longitudinal Evidence from the United States," Sage Open Medicine, July 22, 2016. https://papers.ssrn.com.

What they do not say is that the data behind this statistic is extremely unreliable. According to a report by Dr. Byron Calhoun, vice chair of the Department of Obstetrics and Gynecology of West Virginia University–Charleston, "There are no federal reporting requirements for abortion in the United States. Only 26 states require providers to report. And the data provided are estimates." He asserts that abortion and abortion-related complications are underreported by as much as 50 percent. In addition, he writes that "women experiencing life-threatening health complications from abortion go to hospital's ER's and are not usually seen by abortion doctors and thus their deaths not counted as abortion related." This obscures the fact that there is a very real risk of death from abortion. According to Calhoun, "During 2nd and 3rd trimesters, the abortion related mortality equals and then exceeds that of childbirth."[21] In fact, since abortion was legalized, the Centers for Disease Control and Prevention (CDC) has recorded 424 maternal deaths from legal abortion, two of which occurred in 2011 (the most recent year for which data is available).

In addition to death, there are also serious short- and long-term health risks associated with abortion. A 2014 study by the University of California–San Francisco examined 54,911 abortions and found that 126 "involved major complications, which the researchers defined as conditions that required hospital admission, surgery or a blood transfusion," and that 1,030 "resulted in minor complications in the six weeks following the procedure."[22] Many of these complications affect a woman's future fertility. According to the United Kingdom health care website NHS Choices, after an abortion there is a one-in-ten chance that a woman's uterus will become infected, which can lead to pelvic inflammatory disease and increase the risk of infertility or ectopic pregnancy (when an egg implants inside the fallopian tube instead of the uterus). In addition, up to one in every one hundred surgical abortions results in damage to the cervix, and having several abortions is associated with an increased risk of giving birth prematurely.

> "Having an abortion is not just a walk in the park. There is a possibility of excessive bleeding or injuries and death."[23]
>
> —Freda Bush, an ob-gyn

It is up to the states to mandate that abortion clinics fully inform their patients of these risks, but many states do not have such laws. Dr. Freda Bush, a member of the American Association of Pro-Life Obstetricians and Gynecologists, wonders how many women really understand the risks of abortion. "Having an abortion is not just a walk in the park," she explains. "There is a possibility of excessive bleeding or injuries and death. That means your death. So, I am not confident that when consent is given in an abortion clinic that they are given all of that. . . . Women have definitely been victimized."[23]

Risk to Mental Health

Women who have abortions are also at increased risk of developing serious mental health disorders after the procedure, such as depression and suicidal behavior. This has been well established in scientific studies. For instance, a 2016 study by Dr. D. Paul Sullins of the Catholic University of America found that women who had abortions were significantly more likely to have one or more mental health disorders than women who lost their pregnancies due to miscarriage (45 percent versus 24 percent). The study enrolled more than eight thousand pregnant women and then followed them for over thirteen years, comparing their rates of mental health disorders to rates in the general population. Women who had abortions were 54 percent more likely to suffer from depression, 40 percent more likely to think about suicide, and much more likely to abuse or become dependent on alcohol and drugs (151 percent and 302 percent, respectively). According to Sullins, when all possible outcomes of pregnancy were taken into account, "only abortion was consistently associated with higher risk of mental disorder."[24]

The reason abortion is so detrimental to mental health is fairly obvious: Deliberately ending the life of one's offspring will naturally cause negative emotions. These feelings are well documented in the medical text *A Clinician's Guide to Medical and Surgical Abortion*, which lists depression, guilt, shame, regret, and grief as the most common emotions. Some studies have attempted to minimize these very natural reactions by attributing them to feelings of stigma about abortion or a perceived need for secrecy. In other words, they attribute the cause of the negative feelings to society rather than to the abortion itself. Pro-life Christian writer Anthony Crescio believes this distinction is meaningless. "The conscience of the woman is telling her that . . . by rejecting the child, she has rejected life in general and she feels the need to hide this from those around her,"[25] he writes. In other words, women who have an abortion realize—consciously or unconsciously—that rejecting life is an unnatural act. That act has the potential to do great harm on a moral or spiritual level, harm that often manifests as mental health disorders or substance abuse.

Unfortunately, modern society also perpetuates the lie that abortion is a perfectly reasonable choice. It is reasonable, society says, because the burden of caring for a child can diminish the life of a woman, who must give up her dreams and become, as society often puts it, "just a mother." Abortion plays into this idea, pitting women against their unborn children—at great cost to both. Crescio argues that pro-choice advocates must help women see that "far from being a burden . . . , motherhood is an opportunity, of 'Biblical proportions' if you will, . . . to grow as a human person."[26]

Adoption Is the Answer

For a variety of reasons, motherhood is not the right choice for everyone. Children need mature, emotionally and financially stable parents to thrive, and many women who choose abortion do so because they do not believe they can properly care for their child. But abortion is not the only option. There is no shortage of loving and able parents waiting to adopt newborn infants. Considering the physical, mental, and spiritual risks of abortion, adoption is the choice with the best long-term outcome. According to Laurel Shaler, assistant professor of counselor education and family studies at Liberty University, "Through adoption, women have an amazing opportunity to redeem a bad decision or unintended consequence."[27] Adoption allows women the comfort of knowing that they gave their child the best possible future.

> "The conscience of the woman is telling her that . . . by rejecting the child, she has rejected life in general and she feels the need to hide this from those around her."[25]
>
> —Anthony Crescio, pro-life Christian writer

The most effective way to protect women from the harms of abortion is to make sure adoption is a viable option. Unfortunately, only about fourteen thousand newborns are adopted each year in the United States, a number that has remained steady for about twenty years. In contrast, over 1 million abortions are performed each year. In many cases, women do not choose adoption because they fear the feelings of grief they may experience when giving their child to another. Supporting these women through the process and validating their choice is the best way to protect them from the grave health issues associated with abortion.

Abortion is never the best choice for a woman. Pro-life groups offer a myriad of resources to women who choose to bring their pregnancies to term, from counseling and financial assistance to adoption services. In order to avoid the threats to their physical, mental, and spiritual health, women must make the choice that honors their unique abilities: They must choose life.

Abortion Is Not Harmful to Women

"An abortion when needed will always be—as it was for my family—a blessing, a mercy, the gift of a fresh start, and a renewed opportunity for life to flourish."

—Psychologist Valerie Tarico

Valerie Tarico, "4 Ways to Change the Conversation About Abortion: Start with Talking About What Comes After," *Salon*, September 3, 2015. www.salon.com.

Consider these questions as you read:

1. If abortion was banned, do you worry that women would turn to illegal abortion? Why or why not?
2. Do you agree with the essay that most women who choose abortion are making the best choice for themselves and their families? Explain your reasoning.
3. In your opinion, is it okay for women to have an abortion so they can pursue a future of their choice? Use examples from the text to support your answer.

Editor's note: The discussion that follows presents common arguments made in support of this perspective, reinforced by facts, quotes, and examples taken from various sources.

Women suffer when they are denied reproductive choice. They suffer physically and financially, and they are forced to live out a future they did not want. Countless studies have shown that women who choose abortion have better outcomes than women who are forced to give birth to unwanted children and that legalizing abortion has improved the lives of women of all stations.

Abortion Is Safer than Pregnancy

There is widespread agreement among medical professionals that first trimester abortion is one of the safest medical procedures in existence.

A 2015 study of 667 women who received abortions found that the overwhelming majority believed that terminating their pregnancies was the right decision for them. The women reported their current feelings about their abortions every six months for a period of three years. At each point, more than 99 percent maintained that they believed getting an abortion had been the right decision. The study confirms that women who get abortions do not regret their decisions and know what is best for themselves and their families.

99% Women who say abortion was the right decision

Women who say abortion was the wrong decision **1%**

Source: C.H. Rocca et al., "Decision Rightness and Emotional Responses to Abortion in the United States: A Longitudinal Study," PLoS ONE, July 8, 2015. http://journals.plos.org.

In fact, it is even safer than carrying a pregnancy to term. According to the Guttmacher Institute, only five women out of one thousand, or 0.05 percent, who have a first trimester abortion have a major complication that might require hospitalization. When all legal abortions are taken into account, abortion is still much safer than pregnancy. A 2012 study that surveyed data from the CDC and other reputable sources found that overall there were 0.6 maternal deaths per 100,000 legal abortions performed in the United States, compared to 8.8 deaths per 100,000 live births. According to the study's authors, "Legal induced abortion is markedly safer than childbirth. The risk of death associated with child-birth is approximately 14 times higher than that with abortion."[28]

The long-term health effects of abortion are also minimal. Research-ers have found that there is almost no risk of developing infertility after a woman has a first trimester abortion, nor is it more likely that a woman who becomes pregnant later will have an ectopic pregnancy, have a mis-carriage, or give birth to a low-weight or preterm baby. And according to the American Cancer Society, there is no cause-and-effect relationship between abortion and an increased risk of breast cancer.

Dangers of Illegal Abortion

However, there is ample evidence that if abortion were made illegal once again, most women who experience an unwanted pregnancy would still seek one out—but illegally. David Grimes of the CDC found that as many as 1.2 million illegal abortions were performed in the United States each year in the 1950s, when abortion was illegal. This means that, at a time when the US population was much lower than it is today, the number of illegal abortions was higher than the current number of legal abortions. This implies that outlawing abortion will by no means reduce its occurrence. Women who turn to illegal abortion risk deadly infec-tion or physical damage that requires emergency surgery. According to Grimes, "When denied access to safe, legal abortion, desperate women will risk their lives to control their fertility. Many will die as a result."[29] He estimates that more than one thousand women died each year in the 1940s from illegal abortions and countless more were hospitalized. If abortions were once again illegal and women had no recourse but to seek out illegal ones, the cost in human suffering, and perhaps even human life, would be horrifying.

Laws restricting abortion are already causing some women to seek out an illegal abortion. According to the Texas Policy Evaluation Proj-ect, in recent years 100,000 to 250,000 Texas women chose an illegal abortion method because of the barriers to legal abortion in their state. Methods included drug-induced abortion, taking herbs, getting hit or punched in the abdomen, using alcohol or drugs, or taking hormonal pills. It is likely that most of these women felt they had no choice but to terminate their pregnancies, regardless of the health risks to themselves. To protect such women, all localities need reasonable access to safe and affordable abortion services.

Choice Leads to Better Outcomes

When it comes to abortion, women know what is best for themselves and their families. Studies have shown that women who receive abortions do better in almost every respect when compared to women who want an abortion but cannot get one. "When you ask women why they want an abortion, they tell you that they want it because they don't have enough money to raise a child, that their relationship with the man involved isn't good, and that they need to take care of the kids they already have,"[30] explains Diana Foster, a researcher at the University of California–San Francisco. Foster was one of the architects of the Turnaway Study, a long-term research project on the effects of abortion restriction. The study found that women who were granted abortions were better off financially and had better relationships than those who were forced to carry their pregnancy to term.

The Turnaway Study also found that women who have abortions take better care of the children they already have. According to the Guttmacher Institute, 61 percent of women in the United States who have abortions already have children, and most say they want to terminate their pregnancies because they cannot properly care for another child. Preliminary data from the Turnaway Study seems to confirm this; in general, the children of women who were denied abortions did worse, in terms of child development, than the children of women who received abortions. Foster says this explains why the

> "When you ask women why they want an abortion, they tell you that they want it because they don't have enough money to raise a child, that their relationship with the man involved isn't good, and that they need to take care of the kids they already have."[30]
>
> —Diana Foster, researcher at the University of California–San Francisco

primary emotion the women reported feeling after receiving an abortion was relief. According to Foster, these women are "making decisions that are good for them"[31] and their families.

Abortion Gives Women a Chance to Thrive

Legalizing abortion has allowed countless women to pursue their dreams and contribute to society. For so many years, becoming pregnant meant a woman was destined to become a primary caregiver, regardless of her talents or aspirations. Today an unwanted pregnancy does not have to determine the course of a woman's life. "*Roe v. Wade* meant a future I could control," explains K, who had an abortion when she was sixteen. As she tells the *Huffington Post*, if abortion had not been an option, "I probably would have been stuck in the little town where I grew up, no college, having to work really hard to raise him. Instead, I've gone to school, got a graduate degree, I run a non-profit and do a lot of work with the environment. I'm able to do those things, because I was able to make that decision."[32]

> "*Roe v. Wade* meant a future I could control."[32]
>
> —K, who had an abortion at age sixteen

Teens rarely have the maturity or the financial resources to raise a child. While the rate of teen pregnancy is dropping, 553,000 girls aged fifteen to nineteen became pregnant in 2011. It is more difficult for teens to get abortions than older women—teens have fewer financial resources, and those who live in states that have parental consent laws are sometimes too afraid to tell a parent they are pregnant early in their pregnancy. If the many barriers to abortion were removed for teens, more teen girls would be able to delay childbearing until they have the maturity and financial resources to raise a child. According to psychologist Valerie Tarico, the opportunity to choose when one has a child can lead to "a high school graduation ceremony, a receptionist job that is a first step out of poverty, a Peace Corps volunteer teaching in Africa, a stable loving partnership that comes when the time is right, and the chosen child born to the mom who waited."[33] Because of abortion, many girls will get to go to college, start a business, do humanitarian work, or otherwise contribute to society. And if they later choose to become mothers, they can do so as mature, financially secure adults.

Abortion is never ideal. But women deserve to be able to determine their own destinies. They cannot reach their potential as human beings unless they have control over their bodies, their fertility, and their futures. Women and their doctors are the ones best able to make the complex, difficult, and emotional decision about whether to have an abortion.

Chapter Three

Is Abortion Harmful to Society?

Abortion Is Harmful to Society

- Because of abortion, society has been deprived of the contributions of millions of people.
- Abortion erodes diversity by disproportionately affecting minorities.
- Abortion threatens society's moral code by devaluing human life.

The Debate at a Glance

Abortion Is Not Harmful to Society

- The cost of unwanted pregnancy has a substantial effect on society.
- Abortion helps women and their families escape the cycle of poverty.
- Unwanted children face many challenges that make it more difficult for them to contribute to society.

Abortion Is Harmful to Society

"I cannot help but wonder what our society might look like were it not for abortion; would a cure for cancer have been developed?"

—Laurel Shaler, assistant professor at Liberty University in Lynchburg, Virginia

Laurel Shaler, "3 Ways Abortion Robs America's Mothers—and All of Us," *Bound4LIFE* (blog), May 3, 2016. http://bound4life.com.

Consider these questions as you read:

1. How persuasive is the argument that abortion has negatively impacted America financially? Explain your reasoning.
2. One argument made in this essay is that America has lost talented—and perhaps extraordinary—people because of abortion. Do you think this is a convincing argument against abortion? Why or why not?
3. What do you think is meant by *racial genocide* as it applies to abortion?

Editor's note: The discussion that follows presents common arguments made in support of this perspective, reinforced by facts, quotes, and examples taken from various sources.

Since *Roe v. Wade* made abortion legal in 1973, over 58 million unborn children have been aborted in the United States—a staggering number of human lives lost. This loss of human potential has had a profound effect on American society—financially, culturally, and morally.

Destinies Lost

Americans believe in an unalienable right to life, liberty, and the pursuit of happiness for a very good reason: A society that respects self-determination allows humans to reach their full potential. Yet the millions of fetuses that have been aborted in the United States never had an opportunity to reach their potential—or to share their gifts with society. This loss of human potential is overwhelming. Of course, there is no way to know if one of these children would have invented a revolutionary clean energy source, solved world hunger, or ended a war. But many would have surely enriched society, growing up to be teachers, doctors, first responders, conservationists, or simply loving parents, raising and nurturing the next generation. Unfortunately, society will never know the gifts and contributions it has lost.

However, by looking at the ways in which children whose mothers chose adoption have enriched the world, one can get an idea of the scope of this lost potential. For instance, American artist Faith Hill's remarkable talents were allowed to flourish because her mother chose adoption over abortion. Hill, who is one of the most successful country artists of all time, is also a noted philanthropist, funding children's literacy projects and raising millions for the survivors of natural disasters such as Hurricane Katrina, which devastated New Orleans in 2005. "I know she [my birth mother] must have had a lot of love for me to want to give me what she felt was a better chance," she says. "How thankful I am that she was able to give me the opportunity that I had. I was placed into an incredible home that . . . is responsible for the way I am today."[34]

> **"I'm glad I didn't end up as an abortion."[35]**
>
> —Steve Jobs, cofounder and CEO of Apple

Another remarkable person whose mother chose adoption was Steve Jobs, the cofounder of the computer company Apple. Jobs's revolutionary creations (such as the iPhone and the iPad) changed the way that humans interact with computers. His biographer Walter Isaacson reports that before Jobs passed away in 2011, he expressed gratitude toward his birth mother, Joanne Schieble. "I wanted to . . . thank her, because I'm glad I didn't end up as an abortion," Jobs said. "She was 23 and she went through a lot to have me."[35]

Jobs, Hill, and countless others have contributed to society in innumerable ways—all because they were allowed to live, grow, and reach their potential. By denying this right to so many millions, society is squandering its greatest resource—its people.

Abortion Rate by Racial/Ethnic Group in New York City

In 2016 the New York City Department of Health and Mental Hygiene reported that rates of abortion in 2014 among African Americans and Hispanics were over four times and two times higher, respectively, than the rate among whites. The department also found that, in 2014, more African American fetuses were aborted in New York City (27,367) than there were African American live births (23,680). Pro-life advocates say these results substantially decrease minority populations, which harms society.

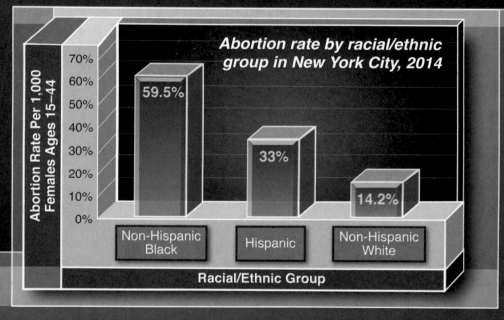

Abortion rate by racial/ethnic group in New York City, 2014

- Non-Hispanic Black: 59.5%
- Hispanic: 33%
- Non-Hispanic White: 14.2%

Abortion Rate Per 1,000 Females Ages 15–44

Racial/Ethnic Group

Source: New York City Department of Health and Mental Hygiene, Office of Vital Statistics, *Summary of Vital Statistics*, 2014. New York, NY, 2016. www.1.nyc.gov.

The Financial Impact of Abortion

This loss of American citizenry also has a profound economic impact on society. Societies need people to contribute financially, and with 58 million lives lost to abortion in the United States since *Roe v. Wade*, a huge percentage of the population is simply missing. According to family trends expert Glenn Stanton, babies are essential to a nation's financial health. "Economic growth, debt retirement and support of an increasing population of elderly requires young workers," he explains, "and these young creators, providers, inventors, consumers—not to mention taxpayers—only come in one original size: babies."[36]

Mark Olson, a political scientist and pro-life political consultant, has calculated the loss in federal tax revenue due to abortion. He estimates that, if abortions performed before *Roe v. Wade* are taken into account, by 2010 about 117 million abortions had taken place in the United States, with a loss in tax revenue of $12.3 trillion. As he writes in the promotional material for his 2014 book, *Abolition*, "A nation's economy cannot be sustained when nearly one-third of its population has been wiped out."[37] Olson has also found that the federal revenue lost due to abortion mirrors the increase in the federal debt over that same period. According to Olson, the massive national debt in the United States is directly related to the fact that natural population growth—which drives the economy—has been stunted by abortion.

Abortion as Racial Genocide

Diversity is perhaps the greatest strength of the United States. Research confirms that when people of diverse backgrounds, races, and abilities work together, businesses are more successful, scientific research is of higher quality, and financial markets are more stable. But abortion weakens diversity by decimating the population of America's minority groups—especially African Americans. The abortion rate among black women is more than four times higher than among white women in the United States. According to Clenard Childress, an African American pastor and the president of Life Education and Resource Network, Northeast,

> "The most dangerous place for an African American is in the womb."[38]
>
> —Clenard Childress, president of Life Education and Resource Network, Northeast

"The most dangerous place for an African American is in the womb." Childress and other pro-life advocates claim that Planned Parenthood is actively targeting black women by concentrating their clinics in minority neighborhoods. They cite these statistics as proof that abortion in America is a form of "racist genocide."[38]

Regardless of whether current abortion policy has been deliberately designed to reduce poor and minority populations, it is clearly having that effect. For instance, in 2014 there were more abortions performed on African American women in New York City (27,367) than there were live births (23,680).

Abortion as Eugenics

Not only does abortion reduce populations among minorities and the poor, it also reduces diversity in society by eliminating fetuses with disabilities. This is a form of eugenics. Eugenics is the science of improving the characteristics of the human species as a whole by controlling who has children. Before it was used by the Nazis in the 1930s and 1940s to justify the genocide of millions of people, eugenics was popular in the United States and led to policies that included mixed-race marriage bans and the forced sterilization of the disabled and mentally ill. After *Roe v. Wade*, many people, including Supreme Court justice Ruth Bader Ginsburg, interpreted it as an extension of the eugenics movement. As Ginsburg said in a 2009 interview, "Frankly I had thought that at the time *Roe [v. Wade]* was decided, there was concern about population growth, and particularly growth in populations that we don't want to have too many of."[39]

States that allow abortion in cases where the unborn child suffers a disability are encouraging eugenic practices. Maria McFadden Maffucci, editor of the pro-life publication *Human Life Review*, believes this sends the message that differently abled people are a drain on society and that their lives are worth less than those of able-bodied people. "It's the arrogance of deciding that someone else's life won't be good enough," she says. By not allowing differently abled babies to be born, society cannot benefit from their contributions. The practice also devalues life in general—a dangerous practice for any society. "If one group of humans can be killed, then *any* group of humans can be killed," she says. "It only depends on who's in power, who's deciding which group to kill. That *ought* to scare people."[40]

The loss of so many millions of lives to abortion has weakened America. It has made this country poorer, less innovative, less diverse, and less ethical. The inclusion of all is good for society as a whole. But this means including everyone, especially the unborn—who are, quite literally, America's future.

Abortion Is Not Harmful to Society

"Denying abortion is linked to social maladjustment, delinquency, crime, alcoholism, under-employment, and poverty."

—David Grimes, former chief of the Abortion Surveillance Branch at the CDC

David Grimes, "Abortion Denied: Consequences for Mother and Child," *Huffington Post*, June 2, 2015. www.huffingtonpost.com.

Consider these questions as you read:

1. Taking into account the facts and ideas presented in this discussion, how persuasive is the argument that abortion ultimately benefits society? Which arguments are strongest and why?
2. Do you think abortion is justified if a woman cannot afford to have a child? Why or why not?
3. What do you think is meant by the term *unproductive adult* in relation to abortion?

Editor's note: The discussion that follows presents common arguments made in support of this perspective, reinforced by facts, quotes, and examples taken from various sources.

When women have the freedom to plan their families, everyone benefits. When they do not—when women are forced to bear children for whom they are unable to properly care—society suffers. Billions of tax dollars are spent supporting unplanned pregnancies and related services. Families become trapped in a cycle of poverty, and unwanted children often grow up to become unproductive adults. Making sure that all women have access to safe and affordable abortion services is the best way to strengthen the American family—which in turn strengthens society as a whole.

Cost of Abortion Restrictions

Many pro-life advocates believe that all pregnancies—whether they are intended or not—should be carried to term. But when women cannot afford to pay for prenatal care and delivery, society is forced to pick up the tab. This puts a tremendous strain on Medicaid and other public health programs paid for with tax dollars. According to the Guttmacher Institute, in 2010 (the most recent year for which national statistics are available) the public paid about $21 billion in pregnancy-related costs for about 2 million births. Of the approximately 1 million women who terminated their pregnancies, three-fourths stated they did so out of financial necessity. If these women were instead forced to carry those pregnancies to term, the cost to the public would increase by as much as tens of billions of dollars in prenatal care and hospital delivery costs.

There is an additional cost to the public if a fetus is found to have health problems. Many times such problems cannot be detected until after abortion becomes illegal (usually between twenty and twenty-four weeks, depending on the state). This means that many parents who learn that their child will be born with a debilitating—or even fatal—health issue cannot terminate the pregnancy in the state in which they live. Lower-income women who cannot afford to travel to another state are disproportionately affected by these bans. Some of these children have no chance of survival and die shortly after birth—often in agony. Others have such profound deformities that they will live short, agonizing lives. For those who survive, even briefly, health care costs can be astronomical.

The horror posed by the Zika virus (a mosquito-borne virus that causes catastrophic birth defects in developing fetuses) is an example of the enormous social and financial costs that can result from bans on abortion. Many fetuses infected with Zika develop microcephaly—a defect that leaves newborns with small skulls, malformed brains, and severe developmental problems. Children with Zika often have a poor quality of life: They struggle to see, hear, and eat, and some are only alert for one hour a day. Caring for such children is also extremely expensive. The CDC has estimated that a child born with congenital Zika syndrome requires up to $10 million in health care spending over his or her lifetime.

Low-Income Women Who Are Denied Abortions Struggle Financially

From 2010 to 2015, the Turnaway Study tracked one thousand low-income women who sought abortions. The study compared those who received an abortion to those who were denied one. The latter group, called turnaways, were unable to obtain abortions because their pregnancies were too advanced—often because they were unable to make financial or travel arrangements sooner and missed the legal threshold to receive an abortion. The study found that, one year after being denied an abortion, turnaways were less likely to be working full time, and were more likely to be living below the federal poverty level and relying on public assistance. The study confirms that denying abortion increases poverty and makes it more difficult for women to become productive members of society.

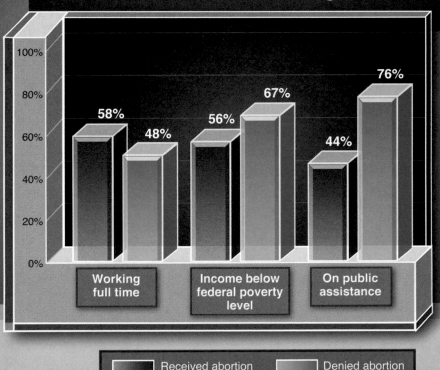

Financial Status One Year After Seeking an Abortion

	Working full time	Income below federal poverty level	On public assistance
Received abortion	58%	56%	44%
Denied abortion	48%	67%	76%

Received abortion   Denied abortion

Source: Renuka Nagaraj, *Securing Autonomy: The Link Between Reproductive Health Access and Financial Security*, Progressive Congress, 2016, p. 7. https://static1.squarespace.com.

As of July 2016 nearly 540 pregnant women in the United States were infected with the Zika virus. Congenital Zika syndrome often cannot be detected in a fetus before twenty weeks, the cutoff date for abortion in eighteen states. This means that some fetuses with Zika will have to be brought to term and then kept alive by extraordinary means at an astronomical cost, regardless of that child's suffering and/or the wishes of the parents. According to Sasha Bruce of NARAL Pro-Choice America, "Women deserve a full range of health care options, including abortion. . . . This is true always, but especially during a public health crisis."[41]

Denying Abortion Traps Women in Poverty

Denying women abortion services has other long-term costs on society. For some women, having an unwanted child traps them in a cycle of poverty they cannot escape, and they must rely on public assistance to survive. The vast majority of women who seek abortions already live at or near the federal poverty level (FPL). In 2014, 49 percent of abortion patients had incomes below the FPL (in 2014 that was $11,670 for a single adult), and 26 percent had incomes of 100 percent to 199 percent of the FPL. According to the Guttmacher Institute, three-fourths of all women who seek abortions say they are doing so because their income is too low or because they already have children and cannot afford another.

> "Women deserve a full range of health care options, including abortion . . . especially during a public health crisis."[41]
>
> —Sasha Bruce, NARAL Pro-Choice America

In addition, many of these women are so poor that they must delay their abortions because they need time to raise funds to pay for them. In a 2015 publication, Planned Parenthood notes that 36 percent of women who have second trimester abortions (after twelve weeks) did so because they needed time to raise money for the procedure—the cost of which increases with gestational age. It is difficult to imagine that a woman who cannot pay for an abortion, which varies from about $500 at ten weeks' gestation to $1,500 at twenty weeks' gestation, would not be trapped in poverty if she then had to pay for diapers, formula, clothing, child care, and the myriad of other expenses that go with raising a child. When abortion is not available to these women, they are forced to care for their families by relying on social programs funded with tax dollars.

Studies confirm this. For instance, the Turnaway Study found that low-income women who are denied abortions and give birth to unwanted children are worse off financially than those who are granted abortions. The two groups the study compared started on the same financial footing, but one year later the women who had been denied abortions were more likely to receive public assistance and have household incomes below the FPL. They were also less likely to be working full time, making them less able to contribute to society. According to David Grimes, former head of the Abortion Surveillance Branch at the CDC, this data confirms that "denying women abortion can send them and their children spiraling into economic deprivation."[42]

> "Denying women abortion can send them and their children spiraling into economic deprivation."[42]
>
> —David Grimes, former head of the Abortion Surveillance Branch at the CDC

Unwanted Children Become Unproductive Adults

When a mother is forced to raise a child she does not want, there is a very good chance that the child—and society as a whole—will suffer for it. Unwanted children face many challenges that can impact how they function in society later in life. For instance, a landmark 1966 Swedish study that followed 120 unwanted children (children born after their mothers were denied abortion) for thirty-five years found that unwanted children were twice as likely to be hospitalized for mental illness, three times as likely to commit crimes, and six times as likely to receive public assistance. Later studies have similar findings, including a 1997 study published in the medical journal *Pediatrics* that found that children born to unwed teenagers were eleven times more likely to become chronic juvenile delinquents. Children like these—who are raised by mothers who are still children themselves—rarely receive the tools and support they need to become productive members of society. Society cannot provide those tools and support—only loving, stable families can.

It may sound callous to argue that abortion is good for society. But society thrives when it is made up of self-sufficient, productive individuals. This is only possible when children are wanted and loved, when women can determine their own destinies, and when families can support themselves. Strong, self-sufficient families are the foundation of a strong society, and family planning—including abortion—makes strong families possible.

Chapter Four

Are Laws Regulating Abortion Adequate?

Laws That Regulate Abortion Are Too Permissive

- D&E abortion is a brutal procedure that should not be legal to perform on healthy fetuses that are capable of feeling pain.
- Federal law does not require fetuses to be anesthetized before abortion, even though surgeons routinely anesthetize fetuses before surgery in the womb.
- Federal law allows women to abort fetuses with minor disabilities, even though children born with these disabilities can have a good quality of life.

The Debate at a Glance

Laws That Regulate Abortion Are Too Restrictive

- Many laws regulating abortion are intended to dissuade women from going through with the procedure.
- Some abortion regulations mandate that doctors perform procedures that are medically unnecessary.
- Laws that hold abortion clinics to unnecessarily strict health care standards force many of them to close, which makes abortion much more difficult for women to obtain and is a violation of their rights.

Laws That Regulate Abortion Are Too Permissive

"Science has expanded our knowledge of unborn pain, and it's time for the law to catch up. . . . What kind of inhumane culture gives 'wanted' babies anesthesia but tortures others? Sadly, ours."

—Tony Perkins, president of the Family Research Council, a Christian lobbying organization

Tony Perkins, "Womb for Improvement in Abortion Law," Family Research Council, March 16, 2016. www.frc.org.

Consider these questions as you read:

1. What facts presented here support the idea that some types of abortion should be banned? Explain your answer.
2. How should the argument that fetuses feel pain during the abortion procedure affect federal abortion law, if at all? Explain your answer.
3. Do you think states should have the right to ban abortion when the fetus is disabled? Explain your reasoning.

Editor's note: The discussion that follows presents common arguments made in support of this perspective, reinforced by facts, quotes, and examples taken from various sources.

Most pro-life advocates believe that the most morally reprehensible part of *Roe v. Wade* is that it allows abortion up to fetal viability. This means that some abortions are performed on fetuses that are so far along in their development that they can actually feel the pain caused by the procedure. This is further unacceptable when one considers that many of these fetuses are either completely healthy or have only a minor disability. Current law is far too permissive in allowing abortion on demand in the later months of pregnancy, and the practice must be stopped.

Why Restrict Abortion After the First Trimester?

To understand why pro-life advocates are so passionately against abortion after the first trimester, one must first understand how most of these abortions are performed. Once the fetus is too large to be extracted from the uterus using vacuum aspiration—which occurs at some point during the fourth month of pregnancy—a D&E abortion is performed. In this procedure, the abortion provider dilates the cervix, drains the amniotic fluid that surrounds the fetus, and then extracts the fetus using a method described by Supreme Court justice Anthony Kennedy in the following way:

> A doctor inserts grasping forceps through the woman's cervix and into the uterus to grab a living fetus. The doctor grips a fetal part with the forceps and pulls it back through the cervix and vagina, continuing to pull even after meeting resistance from the cervix. The friction causes the fetus to tear apart. For example, a leg might be ripped off the fetus as it is pulled through the cervix and out of the woman. The fetus, in many cases, dies just as a human adult or child would: It bleeds to death as it is torn apart limb by limb. The fetus can be alive at the beginning of the dismemberment process and can survive for a time while its limbs are being torn off.[43]

Using statistics from the Guttmacher Institute and the National Abortion Federation, pro-life advocates estimate that the D&E procedure is used in about 10 percent of abortions each year, which means more than one hundred thousand fetuses are killed in this way. There is widespread agreement about the brutality of the procedure, especially since it is performed on fetuses three to six months of gestational age. "Before the first trimester ends, the unborn child has a beating heart, brain waves, and every organ system in place," explains National Right to Life's director of state legislation Mary Spaulding Balch. "Dismemberment abortions occur after the baby has reached these milestones."[44] Balch was one of many who supported an Alabama law to ban the procedure. That law passed in May 2016, but it was blocked by a federal judge in October, who claimed the law was likely unconstitutional. According to Bill Klein, president of Alabama Citizens for Life, "Alabama children should be protected by law from being torn limb from limb. No human should die this way in a civilized society."[45] However, as of 2016 only four states had successfully banned the procedure.

Fetuses Can Feel Pain in the Second Trimester

The main reason to ban D&E abortions—or any abortion after about eighteen weeks' gestation—is because it is at this point that a fetus feels pain. This is a well-established fact in medical science. According to Montana state representative Albert Olszewski, a practicing orthopedic surgeon, "Starting at 18 to 20 weeks, you can say with empirical certitude that there are physiological responses to pain."[46] These responses have been studied by doctors who perform surgeries on fetuses while they are in the womb. These surgeons have observed fetuses flinching and moving away from painful stimuli. They note the fetuses' bodies are often flooded by stress hormones like cortisol, which humans produce in response to pain. According to Elaina Lin, an anesthesiologist who specializes in fetal anesthesia techniques, "By the late second or early third trimester, what most clinicians can agree on is that the pathways are there for them to feel some sort of stimulation."[47] Because of this, surgeons routinely administer anesthesia to fetuses before surgery to keep them still and to prevent any physiological pain response that would interfere with healing.

> "Alabama children should be protected by law from being torn limb from limb. No human should die this way in a civilized society."[45]
>
> —Bill Klein, president of Alabama Citizens for Life

Pro-choice advocates question whether a fetus's brain is developed enough to interpret these sensations as pain. They insist that a fetus's neural pathways in the cerebral cortex—the part of the brain associated with higher brain function such as thought—are not developed enough to process pain. However, scientists note that pain is a fundamental survival mechanism present in animals without cerebral cortexes. Maureen

Many Americans Want Stricter Limits on Abortion

Many Americans believe *Roe v. Wade*, which gives women the right to abortion-on-demand up until fetal viability, is too permissive. A 2016 survey of 1,009 adults by the Marist Institute for Public Opinion found that 78 percent wanted stricter limits on the circumstances under which abortion is legal. The largest percentage of respondents, for instance, stated that abortion should only be permitted in a case of rape or incest or to save the life of the mother.

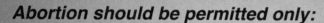

Abortion should be permitted only:

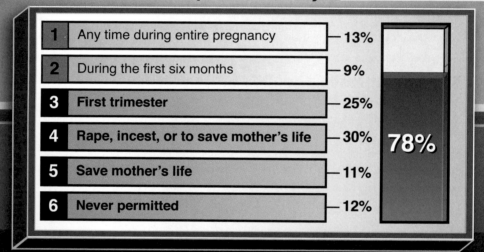

1	Any time during entire pregnancy	13%
2	During the first six months	9%
3	First trimester	25%
4	Rape, incest, or to save mother's life	30%
5	Save mother's life	11%
6	Never permitted	12%

78%

Source: Knights of Columbus, "Americans Support Abortion Restrictions," 2016. www.kofc.org.

Condic, an associate professor of neurobiology and anatomy at the University of Utah, points out that animals without cerebral cortexes still seem to suffer from pain. She asks, "If you chopped a wing off of a live chicken and it ran around squawking and flapping its wing frantically and ran away from you, is it suffering? If we wouldn't do that, if we wouldn't approve of a little kid who tortures a fish by tearing off its fins, how can we argue that a fetus can't suffer?"[48]

Condic was speaking in support of a Utah law that would require a woman to receive general anesthesia for abortions performed at twenty weeks or later, a procedure that would also anesthetize the fetus. Other laws have attempted to require that a fetus receive anesthesia directly or that abortions be banned at or around twenty weeks, when there is strong evidence that a fetus can feel pain. These laws are under attack by pro-choice groups, and several have been struck down by federal judges.

Aborting Disabled Children Should Be Banned

Roe v. Wade also allows women to abort fetuses because they have a disability. Pro-choice advocates call this a kindness, saying it saves these children and their families from a lifetime of suffering. Many of these disabilities are not life-threatening, however, and children with comparable disabilities go on to live productive, happy lives. For instance, children with Down syndrome have physical and intellectual disabilities that can be mild, and many people with Down syndrome integrate easily into society. Mark Leach, an attorney who writes about ethical concerns surrounding Down syndrome, believes the syndrome is simply "one more expression of humanity."[49]

Yet fetuses with Down syndrome are being aborted at alarming rates. For instance, according to ABC News, about 92 percent of all women who discover they will give birth to a Down syndrome baby decide instead to have an abortion, a practice Leach calls "modern-day eugenics."[50] In addition, because Down syndrome cannot be confirmed until the second trimester, most of these fetuses must endure the pain of a D&E procedure.

> "To my patients, I'd say, 'Yes, this is not what we were expecting—everyone wants to have a healthy child—but now, you know what? That child still has potential for a significant life.'"[51]
>
> —Christina Francis, an ob-gyn in Fort Wayne, Indiana

There is so much concern about the elimination of humans with birth defects that in 2016 Indiana passed a law that banned women from aborting fetuses based solely on a medical diagnosis. "Too often, women learn their baby has Down syndrome and the first thing their physician tells them about is abortion," explained Christina Francis, an ob-gyn in

Fort Wayne, Indiana. "To my patients, I'd say, 'Yes, this is not what we were expecting—everyone wants to have a healthy child—but now, you know what? That child still has potential for a significant life.'"[51] However, as with so many other laws that seek to protect the lives of fetuses, a federal judge blocked the Indiana law before it could be enacted. Until the law is reinstated, fetuses with disabilities will continue to be aborted.

Federal abortion laws are much too permissive, especially in cases of abortion after the first trimester. States must take action to strengthen restrictions on abortion to protect the innocent lives of fetuses in the womb—especially those that are developed enough to experience the excruciating pain caused by abortion.

Laws That Regulate Abortion Are Too Restrictive

"Any right that requires you to take extraordinary measures to access it is no right at all. . . . Not when providers are required by state law to recite misleading information to women to shame and scare them. And not as long as we have laws on the book . . . making it harder for low-income women to exercise their full rights."

—Former senator and secretary of state Hillary Clinton

Quoted in Christina Cauterucci, "Why Hillary Clinton's Call-Out of the Hyde Amendment Is So Important," *Slate*, January 11, 2016. www.slate.com.

Consider these questions as you read:

1. How do state laws discourage women from seeking abortion? Use examples from the text in your answer.
2. If states are permitted to determine standards for health care facilities, why did the Supreme Court rule that the standards Texas placed on its abortion clinics were unconstitutional?
3. Do you think the law should be able to force health care workers to say certain things to their patients? Why or why not?

Editor's note: The discussion that follows presents common arguments made in support of this perspective, reinforced by facts, quotes, and examples taken from various sources.

In recent years there has been a renewed push to limit a woman's legal right to abortion. According to the Guttmacher Institute, 30 percent of all abortion restrictions—or 334 separate measures—have been passed by state legislatures since 2010. Many advocates of these state laws claim that they are intended to make sure women are fully informed about abortion or to protect them from harm from abortion providers. But the true purpose of these laws is clear: to put up barriers and obstacles to abortion. State laws that limit abortion are unnecessarily restrictive, placing an undue and arguably illegal burden on women who seek legal abortion.

Discouraging Women

Many state laws that restrict abortion have the effect of making abortion much more emotionally painful than necessary. One such law is known as forced ultrasound—the requirement that doctors perform an ultrasound on a pregnant woman before an abortion, even if it is not medically necessary. According to the Guttmacher Institute, thirteen states have forced ultrasound laws, and nine require that women be given the option to view the ultrasound and learn about the fetus's development. Critics claim these laws are emotionally manipulative and point out that pro-life policy makers freely admit they are intended to encourage women to change their minds about abortion. Critics also say the laws are designed to shame women in front of their health care providers. Cianti Stewart-Reid, executive director of Planned Parenthood Advocates of Virginia, spoke out about Virginia's forced ultrasound law in 2015. "This law is an appalling and offensive government overreach," she said. "It's not about women's health care; it's about shaming and preventing women from seeking safe, legal health care."[52]

There is also no evidence that these laws reduce abortion. Several studies have shown that viewing an ultrasound rarely persuades a woman to change her mind about abortion. For instance, according to a 2013 study by the Texas Policy Evaluation Project, of the women surveyed in the study, 92 percent said they were sure that they wanted an abortion before—and after—viewing an ultrasound of the fetus.

Mandated counseling laws are also designed to dissuade women from having an abortion. For instance, thirty-five states have laws that require a woman to receive counseling before an abortion is performed, much of which has nothing to do with the medical procedure and is biased toward the pro-life point of view. Six states require that women be

Strict State Laws Reduce Access to Abortion

Before Texas passed HB 2 in 2013—a law that set extreme medical standards for abortion clinics—forty-one abortion clinics were operating in the state. Because of that law, by 2015, eighteen of the state's clinics had closed—leaving only twenty-three clinics clustered in metropolitan areas. Laws like HB 2 place an undue burden on women seeking abortion because it forces them to travel long distances for abortion services.

Texas Abortion Clinics, Before and After Passage of HB 2

Abortion Clinics in 2013

Abortion Clinics in 2015

Source: *New York Times,* "Fewer Abortion Clinics in Texas," June 10, 2015. www.nytimes.com.

informed that personhood begins at conception, which is not a medical concept, and twelve require women to be given information about a fetus's ability to feel pain, which has not been proven by science. Some laws even require doctors to inform women about adoption options or child support options. The American Civil Liberties Union (ACLU) points out that "it is both pointless and cruel to 'inform' a victim of rape or incest that the 'father' of the 'unborn child' is liable for financial assistance if she carries the pregnancy to term."[53] These highly biased laws are designed by pro-life advocates to convince women not to go through with their abortions. They are also disrespectful to women. As the ACLU states, these laws assume "that women do not adequately think through their abortion decision and that the state must do their thinking for them. This assumption reflects a lack of respect for women's moral decision-making."[54] Finally, twenty-seven states require women to wait as long as twenty-four hours between counseling and the abortion procedure so they can think over the information they have received. And fourteen require that counseling be performed in person, which means that women are forced to make two trips to the abortion provider.

Doctors Are Required to Give False Information

Many states also require that doctors provide information about the risks of abortion that have been disproven. According to the Guttmacher Institute, seventeen states require women be counseled about negative effects of abortion that have been debunked by the medical and scientific community, such as an increased risk of becoming infertile, contracting breast cancer, or developing a serious mental health disorder. According to Leah Torres, an ob-gyn in Salt Lake City, Utah, state law mandates that she counsel her patients who are considering abortion about "postabortal syndrome," a condition that does not exist. "There's no such thing," she states. "That's very disturbing for me to have to say, and I have to follow it up with 'This does not exist.' It's got to be confusing for the patient."[55]

Perhaps the most damning proof that these informed consent laws are biased toward the pro-life agenda is the fact that they exist at all. Torres notes that lawmakers do not interfere in the doctor-patient relationships for other, more dangerous medical procedures such as prostate removal surgery or breast augmentation. "None of these other procedures require a physician to read inaccurate information to their patients," she says. "It doesn't happen anywhere else in medicine."[56]

State Laws Close Clinics

Another tactic of pro-life advocates is to encourage states to enact laws that require abortion clinics to have unnecessarily strict standards of care. Even though nine out of ten abortions performed in the United States are medically simple enough to be completed in a clinic or doctor's office, twenty-two states require abortion clinics to meet the same standards as ambulatory surgery centers (ASCs). ASCs are extremely expensive to build and operate. For instance, they must have specialized electrical systems and backup generators, and hallways and doorways must be wide enough to accommodate gurneys and equipment. A single operating room built to ASC standards costs about $1 million, with an additional $500,000 for equipment. Monthly costs for running an ASC clinic are $40,000 higher than a standard clinic.

The result of these laws has been a mass closing of abortion clinics in the United States. *Bloomberg Businessweek* reports that 162 abortion clinics have closed since 2011. Over twenty of these clinics were in Texas, which closed after a 2013 law known as HB 2 was passed. One of the requirements of HB 2 was that abortion clinics meet standards for ASCs. Because of HB 2, fewer than twenty abortion clinics remained in Texas in 2016, and half of those were slated to close when the ASC standards portion of the bill came into effect. The result was that vast areas of Texas were without access to abortion clinics. In 2016 the Supreme Court struck down the Texas law, stating that it placed "a substantial obstacle in the path of women seeking a previability abortion" and "an undue burden on abortion access."[57] However, according to the Guttmacher Institute, as of November 2016, twenty-five states still

> "None of these other procedures require a physician to read inaccurate information to their patients. It doesn't happen anywhere else in medicine."[56]
>
> —Leah Torres, an ob-gyn in Salt Lake City, Utah

regulated abortion clinics to an extent that goes beyond what is medically necessary to ensure a woman's safety.

Abortion Restrictions Hurt Women

Laws that restrict abortion can have dire consequences for women. Women who fear having to undergo state-mandated counseling or who must travel great distances to a clinic may delay abortion. Poor women are particularly vulnerable to delayed abortion because they are most likely to have trouble raising money or arranging transportation in time to receive a medical or vacuum aspiration abortion. Instead, they must get a D&E abortion, which is much more expensive, invasive, and dangerous. A 2015 study published in *Obstetrics & Gynecology* found that the risk of death from abortion increases with the length of a pregnancy, from 0.3 deaths for every 100,000 abortions before eight weeks to 6.7 per 100,000 at eighteen weeks or later.

Other women turn to illegal abortion, a practice that is becoming increasingly prevalent in Texas, where tough laws restricting medical abortion require that women travel to a clinic at least three times to complete the waiting period and abortion process. Instead, many women buy medical abortion drugs from Mexico, where they are available without a prescription. "I hope our politicians are made aware of how many girls are self-aborting in the Rio Grande Valley," says Lester Minto, who runs an abortion clinic in southern Texas. "This law is backfiring."[58]

State laws restricting abortion ultimately hurt women. They interfere with a woman's relationship with her health care provider, restrict access to legal abortion services, and encourage women to seek out illegal abortion. Federal law is clear on abortion, and pro-life advocates must be prevented from attempting to erode *Roe v. Wade* through unconstitutional state legislation.

Source Notes

Overview: Abortion

1. Quoted in Aaron Blake, "The Final Trump-Clinton Debate Transcript, Annotated," *Washington Post*, October 19, 2016. www.washingtonpost.com.
2. Quoted in Blake, "The Final Trump-Clinton Debate Transcript, Annotated."
3. Quoted in Dahlia Lithwick, "The Women Take Over," *Slate*, March 2, 2016. www.slate.com.

Chapter One: Is a Fetus a Person with a Right to Life?

4. Quoted in Abort73.com, "Medical Testimony," October 5, 2015. www.abort73.com.
5. Quoted in Abort73.com, "Medical Testimony."
6. Quoted in Sarah Terzo, "Planned Parenthood Workers: We Lied to Women About the Development of Their Babies," Live Action News, June 13, 2016. http://liveactionnews.org.
7. Quoted in Personhood USA, "8 Horrific Times People Groups Were Denied Their Humanity," July 2, 2014. www.personhood.com.
8. Quoted in United States Holocaust Memorial Museum, "The Murder of the Handicapped." www.ushmm.org.
9. Quoted in Personhood USA, "Peter Singer: It's 'Quite Reasonable' to Kill Infants Under Obamacare," April 24, 2015. www.personhood.com.
10. Quoted in Sarah Zhang, "Why Science Can't Say When a Baby's Life Begins," *Wired*, October 2, 2015. www.wired.com.
11. San Antonio Coalition for Life, "'A Fetus Isn't a Person Until Viability,'" March 7, 2013. http://sacfl.org.
12. Personhood USA, "Education." www.personhood.com.
13. Unborn Victims of Violence Act of 2003, Public Law 108-212, 118 Stat. 568, 2003.
14. Brian Fisher, "Here's How to Stop Any Pro-Choice Argument in Its Tracks," Human Coalition, March 27, 2014. www.humancoalition.org.
15. Adam Gopnik, "Arguing Abortion," *New Yorker*, November 28, 2014. www.newyorker.com.
16. Quoted in Zhang, "Why Science Can't Say When a Baby's Life Begins."
17. Valerie Tarico, "Who Aborts the Most Fertilized Eggs? Families like the Duggars," ValerieTarico.com, January 9, 2015. https://valerietarico.com.
18. Dianne N. Irving, "When Do Human Beings Begin?," OpenRepublic Media, October 6, 2016. http://openrepublic.media.
19. Daniel Fincke, "Moral and Philosophical Arguments Against Fetal Personhood," *Camels with Hammers* (blog), Patheos, June 13, 2014. www.patheos.com.

20. Quoted in Fincke, "Moral and Philosophical Arguments Against Fetal Personhood."

Chapter Two: Is Abortion Harmful to Women?

21. Byron Calhoun, "The Myth That Abortion Is Safer than Childbirth: Through the Looking Glass," *Issues in Law & Medicine*, 2015, pp. 209–212.
22. Quoted in Katie Yoder, "Study: Networks Don't Report Dangers of Abortion to Women," NewsBusters, March 23, 2016. www.newsbusters.org.
23. Quoted in Samuel Smith, "Women Are Dying from Abortion but You Never Hear About It, Says OB-GYN," *Christian Post US*, January 22, 2016. www.christianpost.com.
24. D. Paul Sullins, "Abortion, Substance Abuse, and Mental Health in Early Adulthood: Thirteen-Year Longitudinal Evidence from the United States," Sage Open Medicine, July 22, 2016. https://papers.ssrn.com.
25. Anthony Crescio, "Abortion: A Threat to the Actualization of the Mother," *Human Life Review*, 2015, p. 62.
26. Crescio, "Abortion."
27. Laurel Shaler, "3 Ways Abortion Robs America's Mothers—and All of Us," *Bound4LIFE* (blog), May 3, 2016. http://bound4life.com.
28. Quoted in Irin Carmon, "In Their Own Words: On the Front Lines of the Abortion War," MSNBC, October 19, 2015. www.msnbc.com.
29. David Grimes, "Abortion in Texas: Lessons from Prohibition," *Huffington Post*, June 29, 2016. www.huffingtonpost.com.
30. Quoted in Julia Calderone, "Here's What Happens When Women Are Denied Abortions," Business Insider, December 9, 2015. www.businessinsider.com.
31. Quoted in Calderone, "Here's What Happens When Women Are Denied Abortions."
32. Quoted in Catherine Pearson, "8 Women on Why *Roe v. Wade* Has Mattered So Much to Them," *Huffington Post*, January 22, 2015. www.huffingtonpost.com.
33. Valerie Tarico, "4 Ways to Change the Conversation About Abortion: Start with Talking About What Comes After," *Salon*, September 3, 2015. www.salon.com.

Chapter Three: Is Abortion Harmful to Society?

34. Quoted in Christy Brunke, "Adopting Faith Hill, the Girl They Always Wanted," National Right to Life News Today, December 2, 2015. www.nationalrighttolifenews.org.
35. Quoted in BuzyMummy, "5 Famous People Who Were Almost Aborted," May 19, 2016. www.buzymummy.com.
36. Quoted in Shaler, "3 Ways Abortion Robs America's Mothers—and All of Us."

37. Mark Olson, "'Over $16 Trillion Lost,'" New Clapham Media. http://new clapham.wixsite.com.
38. Quoted in Thomas Williams, "Black Pastor Tells NAACP Abortion Is 'Racist Genocide,'" Breitbart, July 20, 2015. www.breitbart.com.
39. Quoted in Emily Bazelon, "The Place of Women on the Court," *New York Times Magazine*, July 7, 2009. www.nytimes.com.
40. Quoted in Stella Morabito, "*Human Life Review*: Forty Years of Fighting for Human Life and Dignity," *Federalist*, October 21, 2014. http://thefederalist.com.
41. Quoted in Kristen Clark, "Pro-Choice Group Goes After Rubio over Zika, Abortion Rights," *Miami Herald*, September 6, 2016. http://miamiherald.typepad.com.
42. David Grimes, "Abortion Denied: Consequences for Mother and Child," *Huffington Post*, June 2, 2015. www.huffingtonpost.com.

Chapter Four: Are Laws Regulating Abortion Adequate?

43. Quoted in Scott Lloyd, "Banning Dismemberment Abortions: Constitutionality & Politics," *Human Life Review*, 2015, pp. 12–13.
44. Quoted in Steven Ertelt, "Alabama Governor Signs Bill to Ban Dismemberment Abortions Tearing Babies Limb from Limb," LifeNews.com, May 12, 2016. www.lifenews.com.
45. Quoted in Ertelt, "Alabama Governor Signs Bill to Ban Dismemberment Abortions Tearing Babies Limb from Limb."
46. Quoted in Jeff Guo, "Should We Give Fetuses Painkillers Before We Abort Them?," *Washington Post*, March 26, 2015. www.washingtonpost.com.
47. Quoted in Guo, "Should We Give Fetuses Painkillers Before We Abort Them?"
48. Quoted in Micaiah Bilger, "New Utah Law Requires Anesthesia Before Abortion Because Baby Can Feel Intense Pain," LifeNews.com, May 9, 2016. www.lifenews.com.
49. Mark Leach, "Eugenics: Then and Now in the Era of Prenatal Testing for Down Syndrome," Down Syndrome Prenatal Testing, March 31, 2016. www.downsyndromprenataltesting.com.
50. Leach, "Eugenics."
51. Quoted in Danielle Paquette, "Doctors Respond to Indiana Banning Abortions Because of Down Syndrome," *Washington Post*, March 25, 2016. www.washingtonpost.com.
52. Quoted in Laura Bassett, "Virginia Senate Votes to Repeal Ultrasound Mandate," *Huffington Post*, January 23, 2015. www.huffingtonpost.com.
53. American Civil Liberties Union, "Biased Counseling Against Abortion," 2016. www.aclu.org.
54. American Civil Liberties Union, "Biased Counseling Against Abortion."
55. Quoted in Brandy Zadronzy, "Abortion Lies Doctors Are Forced to Tell," *Daily Beast*, March 27, 2015. www.thedailybeast.com.

56. Quoted in Zadronzy, "Abortion Lies Doctors Are Forced to Tell."
57. Quoted in Marina Fang, "Texas Governor Admits Anti-Abortion Law Was About Restricting Abortion," *Huffington Post*, June 27, 2016. www.huffing tonpost.com.
58. Quoted in Lindsay Beyerstein, "Texas Anti-Abortion Law Forces Women to Make Tough Choices," Aljazeera America, January 5, 2014. http://amer ica.aljazeera.com.

Abortion Facts

Facts and Statistics

- The CDC reports that in 2012 there were 13.2 abortions performed for every 1,000 women aged fifteen to forty-four, a decrease of 4 percent from 2011.
- The CDC also reports that in 2012, 20.8 percent of abortions performed at eight weeks' gestation or earlier were medical abortions, an increase of 10 percent from 2011.
- The Hyde Amendment bans the use of federal funds for abortion except to save the life of the mother or in cases of incest or rape. Since 1976 the Hyde Amendment has been added to most federal funding bills.
- According to the Guttmacher Institute, in 2014, 53 percent of abortion patients paid for the procedure themselves, usually because their state had rules preventing the use of state funds for abortion.

Women Who Have Abortions

- According to the CDC, unmarried women had 85.3 percent of all abortions in 2012. Thirty-five percent had already had one or two abortions, and 8.6 had had three or more abortions.
- According to a 2016 study published in the *New England Journal of Medicine*, nearly half of pregnancies among American women are unintended, and about four in ten of these are terminated by abortion.
- The National Abortion Federation reports that African American women were 3.6 times more likely to have an abortion in 2012 than non-Hispanic white women.
- According to the Guttmacher Institute, 51 percent of women having abortions used contraception during the month they became pregnant. In addition, 90 percent of women at risk of unintended pregnancy use contraception.

- The National Abortion Federation reports that the abortion rate of women who also receive Medicaid coverage, a free health care program for needy Americans, is three times as high as that of other women.
- A 2013 study published in *Perspectives on Sexual and Reproductive Health* found that women seeking abortion at or after twenty weeks were less likely to be employed than women seeking early abortion (50 percent versus 33 percent).

Teen Abortion

- According to a 2011 study in *Contraception*, 750,000 teen pregnancies occur each year; 82 percent are unintended, and 35 percent end in abortion.
- According to the Guttmacher Institute, 12 percent of abortion patients in 2014 were teenagers. Eighteen- to nineteen-year-olds accounted for 8 percent of all abortions, fifteen- to seventeen-year-olds for 3 percent, and younger teens for 0.2 percent.
- The CDC reports that in 2012 teens under fifteen had the highest rate of pregnancy that ended in abortion, with 817 abortions for every 1,000 live births.
- According to the website Just Facts, as of 2016 twenty-six states had parental consent laws for minors seeking abortion, and twelve had parental notification laws.
- The Guttmacher Institute reports that 40 percent of minors having an abortion do so without parental consent.

Public Opinion

- According to a 2016 Pew Research Center poll, 49 percent of Americans say that having an abortion is morally wrong, yet only 41 percent say it should be illegal all or most of the time.
- The Pew Research Center also found that in 2016, 84 percent of liberal Democrats said abortion should be legal in all or most cases, while only 30 percent of conservative Republicans believe this.
- The website Just Facts reports that five Gallup Polls conducted from

1992 through 2011 found that 69 percent to 74 percent of adults favor parental consent laws for women under eighteen seeking an abortion.

- According to a 2016 Marist Poll, 62 percent of Americans oppose taxpayer funding for abortions.
- The 2016 Marist Poll also found that 78 percent of Americans want abortion clinics to be held to the same standards as other outpatient surgery centers, and 70 percent want doctors who perform abortions to have admitting privileges to local hospitals.

Related Organizations and Websites

Advancing New Standards in Reproductive Health (ANSIRH)

1330 Broadway, Suite 1100

Oakland, CA 94612

website: www.ansirh.org

The ANSIRH is a research group that conducts social science research on reproduction issues. Its website contains detailed information about the Turnaway Study, a landmark scientific study that compares women who have received abortions to those denied abortions.

Guttmacher Institute

125 Maiden Ln., 7th Floor

New York, NY 10038

website: www.guttmacher.org

The Guttmacher Institute is a pro-choice research and policy organization that provides information about abortion-related studies, analysis, and legislation. Its website contains a wealth of reliable and balanced information used by scientists, lawmakers, and advocates on both sides of the abortion debate.

Human Life Foundation

353 Lexington Ave., Suite 802

New York, NY 10016

website: www.humanlifereview.com

The Human Life Foundation is a pro-life organization that publishes the *Human Life Review*, a journal devoted to promoting right-to-life issues. Its website contains an extensive archive of over forty years of articles and opinion pieces on abortion.

Just Facts

641 Shunpike Rd., #286

Chatham, NJ 07928

website: www.justfacts.com

Just Facts compiles verifiable and unbiased facts about public policy issues. Its section on abortion includes information about human development in the womb, laws and controversies, and statistics and other factual information about abortion.

Live Action

2200 Wilson Blvd., Suite 102, #111

Arlington, VA 22201

website: www.liveaction.org

Live Action is a pro-life advocacy organization dedicated to ending abortion through media dissemination of various undercover investigations into the abortion industry. Its website contains videos, news articles, and information about pro-life issues.

NARAL Pro-Choice America

1156 Fifteenth St. NW, Suite 700

Washington, DC 20005

website: www.prochoiceamerica.org

NARAL is a pro-choice political advocacy organization that works to oppose the restrictions on abortion and advance abortion rights. Its website contains a wealth of information about the legal battles being fought for abortion rights in the United States.

National Abortion Federation (NAF)

1090 Vermont Ave. NW, Suite 1000

Washington, DC 20005

website: https://prochoice.org

The NAF is a pro-choice professional association of abortion providers. Its website provides education, advocacy, and public policy information for women seeking abortion, for providers, and for the public.

National Advocates for Pregnant Women (NAPW)
875 Sixth Ave., Suite 1807
New York, NY 10001
website: http://advocatesforpregnantwomen.org

The NAPW is an advocacy organization that focuses primarily on securing human rights for pregnant and parenting women. It supports abortion rights through legal advocacy and public education. Its website contains articles, fact sheets, and reports about pro-choice issues and women's rights.

National Right to Life Committee (NRLC)
512 Tenth St. NW
Washington, DC 20004
website: www.nrlc.org

The NRLC is the largest and oldest pro-life advocacy and education organization in the United States. Its website contains fact sheets, news, policy information, and a student center.

Personhood USA
website: www.personhood.com
Personhood USA is a Christian pro-life advocacy organization that believes that personhood begins at conception. Its website contains extensive information about the personhood movement and links to essays and scientific studies that support personhood.

For Further Research

Books

Charles Camosy, *Beyond the Abortion Wars: A Way Forward for a New Generation*. Grand Rapids, MI: Eerdmans, 2015.

Ann Furedi, *The Moral Case for Abortion*. Faversham, UK: Palgrave Macmillan, 2016.

David Grimes, *Every Third Woman in America: How Legal Abortion Transformed Our Nation*. Raleigh, NC: Lulu, 2014.

Trent Horn, *Persuasive Pro-Life: How to Talk About Our Culture's Toughest Issue*. El Cajon, CA: Catholic Answers, 2014.

Bertha Alvarez Manninen, *Pro-Life, Pro-Choice: Shared Values in the Abortion Debate*. Nashville, TN: Vanderbilt University Press, 2014.

Katha Pollitt, *Pro: Reclaiming Abortion Rights*. New York: St. Martin's, 2014.

Joshua Wilson, *The New States of Abortion Politics*. Stanford, CA: Stanford University Press, 2016.

Mary Ziegler, *After Roe: The Lost History of the Abortion Debate*. Cambridge, MA: Harvard University Press, 2015.

Internet Sources

Carl A. Anderson, "The Surprising New Normal in the Abortion Debate," *National Review*, January 21, 2016. www.nationalreview.com /article/430127/pro-life-pro-choice-labels-hide-anti-abortion-consensus.

Lindsey Averill, "This Is What It's Really Like to Have a Late-Term Abortion," *Huffington Post*, October 8, 2016. www.huffingtonpost.com /xojane-/this-is-what-its-really-like-to-have-a-late-term-abortion_b_ 8264562.html.

Ken Blackwell, "How the Abortion Tide Turns," *Washington Times*, August 2, 2015. www.washingtontimes.com/news/2015/aug/2/ken-blackwell-americans-becoming-more-pro-life.

Centers for Disease Control and Prevention, *Abortion Surveillance— United States, 2012*, November 27, 2015. www.cdc.gov/mmwr/pdf/ss/ss6410.pdf.

Kurt Eichenwald, "America's Abortion Wars (and How to End Them)," *Newsweek*, December 17, 2015. www.newsweek.com/2015/12/25/abortion-war-overif-you-want-it-be-406137.html.

Index

About the Author

Christine Wilcox writes fiction and nonfiction for young adults and adults. She has worked as an editor, an instructional designer, and a writing instructor. She lives in Richmond, Virginia, with her husband, David, and her son, Doug.